CHINKANA

THE SUBTERRANEAN MYSTERIES OF THE INCAS

IAN DRISCOLL

ISBN 1-478-37363-6

Printed in the United States of America

To Crystal

CONTENTS

1
<u>A KING'S RANSOM</u>

In September of 1532, an illiterate swineherd by the name of Francisco Pizarro led 177 men southward from the Peruvian coastal town of Piura toward Cajamarca, the seat of Atahuallpa, ruler of the Inca Empire.

Fuelled by rumors of vast mines of gold possessed by the Inca kingdom to the south, Pizarro trudged through hundreds of miles of foreign territory, lusting after fame, power and riches. From the various, scattered tribes that he had previously subjugated he'd also learned of the civil war that had recently torn the Inca empire apart, and he was intent upon seeing the newly victorious high Inca in person, in order to assess his strength.

After two months of traveling, in November of the same year, the conquistadors finally arrived at the border of Cajamarca. They found the place entirely deserted, but Pizarro, being anxious to learn of the high Inca's capabilities, as well as his disposition toward the Spanish, chose Hernando de Soto to continue on to Atahuallpa's encampment in order to arrange a formal meeting between the two leaders.

De Soto, accompanied by Pizarro's brother and a handful of cavalry, pressed on in the direction of the Inca camp, until he reached a narrow channel. On the opposite side of the water, he surveyed an enormous fighting force of Inca warriors. Undeterred, the little group of Spanish bandits cautiously forded the stream. The Inca soldiers exhibited no hostility, but instead pointed out the location of their lord, who was seated upon a mat in the middle of a large courtyard, attended by his servants as well as various nobles.

Hernando Pizarro, taking the lead, approached the king and introduced himself to the great Inca, stating that he and the members of his party were subjects of a powerful ruler of a vast empire far across the waters, and that the Spanish had arrived in Peru in order to work with and to serve the Inca. He requested that a meeting be arranged between Atahuallpa and his brother, Francisco Pizarro.

Atahuallpa, through an interpreter, informed the Spanish that he would meet with their captain the following day, after completing a fast. He further told them that they were welcome to take up residence in the vacant public buildings while they awaited his arrival.

Upon returning to the Spanish camp, de Soto and Hernando informed the rest of their company of what had transpired. The Spaniards were particularly interested in the size of the Inca army, which clearly dwarfed their own. Pizarro himself, however, was undaunted. He and his chief officers met that night and decided upon a daring and murderous course of action: they would lure the Inca into a diplomatic meeting where they would ambush and subsequently capture him, thereby cutting off the head of the Inca fighting force and throwing the warriors into disarray.

The following day, the Spanish mercenaries received their orders. They were to lie in wait in the main courtyard, concealing themselves within buildings and behind pillars, and to attack only when they heard the sound of a single gunshot. Then, all at once, they were to spring upon the Inca and his entourage, slaughtering each man without mercy, until Atahuallpa was safely imprisoned.

It was only around mid-morning that the Incas began to move toward the plaza at Cajamarca. Atahuallpa sent word that he would be accompanied by heavily armed soldiers, as the little party of Spanish emissaries had been the day before. As Pizarro could not object to this without raising suspicions, he was compelled to agree, and responded that Atahuallpa had nothing to fear from his men.

Late in the day, however, the Inca force was seen to halt its grand procession, and to begin to make camp roughly a half-mile from the city. Word was sent, informing Pizarro that Atahuallpa intended to spend the night there, and to continue in the morning. Pizarro, worried that a night spent in hiding would rob his troops of their fighting edge, feigned disappointment, saying that all of the evening's entertainment had already been arranged, and that he had been looking forward to dining with the Inca that night.

Upon receiving Pizarro's message, Atahuallpa broke camp and, leaving the majority of his warriors behind, proceeded with roughly 5,000 attendants to the courtyard in Cajamarca, where the Spanish were awaiting his arrival.

As the sun was setting in the West, the high Inca and his attendants filled the square where the bloodthirsty Spanish lay in wait. Father Valverde, a Dominican priest, was the first to approach Atahuallpa, with a bible in hand. He proceeded to tell the Inca monarch about the Catholic church, the Popes and the one true faith of Christianity. As his lengthy speech ended, Atahuallpa inquired as to where he'd heard these things, and by what authority he spoke such words.

Valverde, with exaggerated flash and flair, presented the bible to the Inca, who, after putting the book to his ear and listening for the voice of the Christian God, promptly threw it on the ground, pointing to the sun in the sky and stating: "Your own God, as you say, was put to death by the very men that he created. But my God still lives in the heavens and looks down on his children."

The Dominican, furious over what he considered an unforgivable offense, turned to Pizarro and fairly shouted "Do you not see that while we stand here wasting our breath in talking to this dog, full of pride as he is, the fields are filling with Indians? Set on at once, I absolve you!"

That was, of course, all the excuse that the Spanish required. The mercenaries sprang from their hiding places with a cry, drawing swords and mercilessly striking down the panicked entourage of the high Inca. One after another, nobles and attendants died in their vain efforts to protect the besieged lord. As one was struck down, another took his place in front of the royal litter, attempting to prevent the Spanish from reaching Atahuallpa. Hundreds tried to flee from the square, across the fields to the waiting warriors, but were cut down by Pizarro's cavalry before they could reach the main fighting force. And so it continued, the streets filling with blood, the anguished cries echoing off of the crumbling walls of the packed plaza, until not one of the Inca's five thousand attendants was left alive. Only Atahuallpa himself was spared, as preserving his life was necessary to secure the gold that Pizarro lusted after.

Francisco Pizarro

CHINKANA

Atahuallpa

Hernando Pizarro meets Atahuallpa

Atahuallpa's capture

Save a minor wound that Pizarro himself received due to the carelessness of one of his own men, none of the fewer than 200 Spaniards that joined in the massacre that day were injured.

The plan worked perfectly. Without the divine Atahuallpa to lead them, the Inca generals and troops scattered and disintegrated. The Tahuantinsuyo, the great empire of the Inca, began its long fall into chaos and ruin.

Atahuallpa, for his part, soon realized the true desire of the Spaniards was for the gold that paved the streets, covered the walls, and even lined the gutters of the great Inca capital of Cuzco. He decided to propose a trade: his life for his treasure. He sent word to Pizarro, stating that he would utterly fill the room in which he was being held captive (which measured 17 feet in width by 22 feet in length) with the precious solar metal if only Pizarro would agree to grant him his freedom.

The Spaniards, desirous as they were to secure the treasure they'd killed so many for, readily agreed to the proposal, as they were under no obligation to fulfill their side of the deal once the ransom had been collected.

It took two months, once the orders were dispatched by Atahuallpa, for half of the ransom to be collected in Cuzco and transported to Cajamarca on the backs of thousands of indigenous peasants. The final payload of pure gold weighed an estimated 650 tons, which would today be valued at somewhere in the neighborhood of roughly 5,000,000,000 dollars. Easily one of the greatest ransoms ever paid in the history of civilization.

After receiving the initial payment, the Spanish began to grow impatient. They demanded more, and faster. Atahuallpa, desperate and powerless, only wished to comply, but he could do nothing to speed the arrival of the second half of the treasure being gathered together in Cuzco. And as it happened, fate would intervene. As the rest of the gold was being collected, a translator who had fallen in love with one of Atahuallpa's wives began to spread rumors that the Inca was plotting a revolt, and raising an army to come and slaughter the Spanish.

Unsubstantiated though it was, the rumor provided Pizarro with the excuse he needed to execute the high Inca and solidify his hold on the emperor's territory. Atahuallpa was given a mock trial, promptly found guilty and condemned to death. On the evening of August 29th, 1533, he was tied to a stake and given a choice: either cling to the heathen religion of his forefathers and die in the flames of the pyre, or if he chose to convert and be baptized, the Christians would show mercy and strangle him. He chose the latter, and was garroted to death at dusk. Thus ended the once-great empire of the Inca, brought to nothing by a band of gold-crazed brigands and thieves.

2
<u>Buried In The Bowels Of The Earth</u>

Well, not quite brought to nothing. It's here that the narrative takes a turn for the fantastic, and becomes partially obscured in that ethereal realm between myth and history.

Johann von Tschudi, a nineteenth century explorer and naturalist, reports that once word of the Inca's death reached the loyal attendants of Atahuallpa who were engaged in transporting the rest of the treasure from Cuzco on the backs of 11,000 llamas, they drove the animals off the road and hid the treasure, in an effort to protect it from the insatiable Spanish.

Some particularly noteworthy items among the lost treasure included the gilded mummies of the 13 Incas who had ruled the empire in the past; the enormous golden sun disk, known as the Punchau, that originally decorated one of the walls of the Coricancha - the Temple of the Sun - in Cuzco; a chain of pure gold said to have been 800 feet in length, commissioned by Huayna Capac to commemorate the birth of his son, Huascar; and last but not least, a complete replica of a garden, made of solid gold, which was said to have graced the courtyard of the Coricancha. Cieza de Leon, a Spanish conquistador, writes of this garden:

They also had a garden, the clods of which were made of pieces of fine gold; and it was artificially sown with golden maize, the stalks, as well as the leaves and cobs, being of that metal. They were so well planted, that even when there was a high wind they were not torn up. Besides all this, they had more than twenty golden sheep with their lambs, and the shepherds with their slings and crooks to watch them, all made of the same metal.[1]

This treasure, according to numerous authors, was secreted away and hidden in a vastly ancient tunnel system that was said to stretch from Cuzco, nearly 2000 miles north to Quito in present-day Ecuador; 375 miles south to Tiwanaku, Bolivia; and eastward, into the Madre de Dios region of the Amazon jungle, for an unknown distance. Additional entrances are alleged to be located as far south as the barren Atacama Desert in Chile, and as far east as the small town of Sao Thome das Letras, between Sao Paolo and Rio De Janeiro, Brazil.

The central entrance to this massive network of underground tunnels is said to be located within the fortress of Sacsayhuaman, situated above modern Cuzco, and composed of megalithic blocks that dwarf even the tallest of men, some weighing in excess of 200 tons. This particular tunnel was said to communicate directly with the Coricancha, and to allow the Incas to move between the fortress and their holiest religious site undetected in a time of war.

This entrance, the exact location of which is now lost to time, was called, in the ancient Quechua language of the Inca Empire, "Chinkana", or "the place where one gets lost".

A replica of the Punchau

A golden llama, perhaps similar to those described by de Leon

The author, dwarfed by one of the cyclopean stones that make up Sacsayhuaman

An aerial view of the ruins of Sacsayhuaman

Garcilaso de la Vega, an early historian born of a Spanish father and an Inca mother, writes in his *Royal Commentaries of the Inca* that he and his boyhood friends used to play around the Chinkana in their youth, but never ventured too far for fear of becoming hopelessly lost in the darkness of the tunnels:

> An underground network of passages...was composed of a quantity of streets and alleyways which ran in every direction, and so many doors, all of them identical, that the most experienced man dared not venture into this labyrinth without a guide, consisting of a long thread tied to the first door, which unwound as they advanced. I often went up to the fortress [of Sacsayhuaman] with boys of my own age, when I was a child, and we did not dare to go further than the sunlight itself, we were so afraid of getting lost, after all the Indians had told us on the subject. Since they did not know how to build arches, the roofs of these underground passages were composed of large, flat stones resting on rafters jutting out from the walls.[2]

And Garcilaso was not alone among the early chroniclers to speak of the subterranean structures hidden in and around Cuzco. A Jesuit manuscript dating to 1600, attributes the underground passageway to unknown "Inca kings" and describes its route beneath the city:

> The celebrated cave of Cuzco, called Chinkana by the Indians, was made by the Inca kings. It is very deep, and runs through the center of the city, its mouth or entrance being in the fortress of Sacsayhuaman. It comes down on the side of the mountain where the parish of San Cristobal is situated and, with varying degrees of depth, ends at the Coricancha. All the Incas

to whom I have spoken have told me that the Incas made this costly and laborious cave to enable their kings and armies to go in times of war from the fortress of Sacsayhuaman to the Temple of the Sun to worship their idol Punchau without being detected.

Felipe Guamán Poma de Ayala, a 17th century chronicler, also wrote in his 1615 *New Chronicle and Good Government*, that the entrance to the tunnels, which he specifically referred to as the Chinkana, was to be found in the archaeological site of Sacsayhuaman, describing it as "an opening beneath the earth that reaches to Santo Domingo," referring to the church that was built by the Spanish atop the ruins of the Coricancha.

Father Martin de Murua, in his *Historia general del Piru* (1616), writes of the tunnel system as well, crediting the Inca Tupac Yupanqui – grandfather of Atahuallpa - with its creation, and states that the precise location of the entrance had been lost over time. Additionally, Jesuit Father Agnelio Oliva (1542-1572) mentions the tunnels in passing, attributing them to Huayna Capac, Atahuallpa's father:

> Huayna Capac erected new, very large and sumptuous buildings, and to him is attributed the construction of the underground labyrinth called Chinkana, which communicated with borders, bridges, forts and other edifices.

An early story, often repeated by modern writers, is supposedly found in Pedro del Sancho's *Relacion de la Conquista del Peru* (1534), and though there are numerous question regarding its authenticity, it bears repeating here.[3]

As reported by numerous writers, the chronicler

states that he was approached by an informant who told him that when the Incas ruled Cuzco, he had been held in high esteem by the royal family. Thus, he was privy to certain secrets that other outsiders were not.

The informant, who is never named, stated that when the Spanish invaded the Empire and ruthlessly murdered Atahuallpa, the treasures of the Inca were sealed up in a labyrinthine tunnel system that predated the Incas:

> These treasures were placed in ancient tunnels that were in the land when the Incas arrived. Also placed in these subterranean repositories were artifacts and statues deemed sacred to the Incas. When the hoard had been placed in the tunnels, there was a ceremony conducted by the high priest. Following these rites, the entrance to the tunnels was sealed in such a manner that one could walk within a few feet and never be aware of the entrance.

Del Sancho's informant goes on to inform the Spaniard that he knew the location of the entrance to said tunnels, and that it was near to the place of his birth. Del Sancho, we are told, pressed the informant for further details, but the anonymous man flatly refused, stating that he was "sworn to silence under penalty of death."

Cieza de Leon, a Spanish conquistador, also wrote of the secret system of tunnels in his *Crónicas del Perú*, stating that:

> In many parts of the city there are great edifices under the ground, and even now some tiles and pieces of gold are found buried in the bowels of the earth. Assuredly, there must be great treasure buried within

the circuit of the city, but those who are living know not where to find it.[4]

He relates an exchange between himself and descendants of the Incas, in which the natives demonstrate the vast quantities of gold possessed by, and hidden within, the empire. He reports:

> If all the gold that is buried in Peru, and in these countries, was collected, it would be impossible to count it, so great would be the quantity, and the Spaniards have yet got little compared with what remains. When I was in Cuzco, receiving an account of the Incas from the principal natives, I heard it said...that if all the treasure in the huacas, which are their burial places, was collected together, that which the Spaniards had already taken would look very small, and they compared it to a drop taken out of a great vase of water. In order to make the comparison more striking, they took a large measure of maize, and, dropping one grain out of it, they said, "The Christians have found that; the rest is so concealed that we ourselves do not know the place of it. So vast are the treasures that are lost in these parts..."[5]

He continues:

> ...if when the Spaniards entered [Peru] they had not committed other tricks and had not so soon executed their cruelty in putting Atahuallpa to death, I know not how many great ships would have been required to bring such treasure to Spain as is now lost in the bowels of the earth, and will remain so, because those who buried it are now dead.[6]

---

[1] Cieza, de L. P, and Clements R. Markham. *The Second Part of the Chronicle of Peru*. London: Printed for the Hakluyt Society, 1883. Print. pp.85-86

[2] Vega, Garcilaso , and Maria Jolas. *The Incas: The Royal Commentaries of the Inca*. Arequipa, Peru: Ediciones El Lector, 2008. Print. p.303

[3] The biggest problem with the story is that it appears nowhere within del Sancho's *Relacion*. The first author to tell the story in its present form seems to have been Warren Smith, in his *Lost Cities of the Ancients – Uncovered!* in 1976. Most recently, it was repeated by David Hatcher Childress in his *Lost Cities and Ancient Mysteries of South America*, who cited Smith as his source.

Secondly, even if it were to be found in Sancho's account of the conquest, the chronicle was originally published in 1534, only two years after the death of Atahuallpa. At that time, the Spanish were still scouring the countryside searching for lost gold, and squeezing the Inca's generals for information on hidden stockpiles. Had an informant approached del Sancho with such a story, he most probably would have been seized and tortured until he gave up the information or, more likely, died.

Thirdly, Smith and the authors who have parroted the tale have consistently and incorrectly referred to Pedro del Sancho as a priest, which he was not. In fact, the entire conversation between del Sancho and his informant is usually framed in the context of a confession. But del Sancho was nothing more than Pizarro's secretary, and was not affiliated with the Church in an official capacity. So did Warren Smith simply confuse his sources, or did he make the entire story up in a willful attempt to deceive his readers? We may never know. Luckily, there is a wealth of verifiable testimony from the early chroniclers which does clearly indicate the existence of the mysterious tunnel system under Cuzco.

[4] Cieza, de L. P, and Clements R. Markham. *The Travels of Pedro De Cieza De Leon, A. D. 1532-50, Contained in the First Part of His Chronicle of Peru*. New York: Burt Franklin, 1964. Print. p.331

[5] *Ibid*. p.77

[6] Cieza, de L. P. *The Second Part of the Chronicle of Peru*. p.41

3
THE GODS OF THE DEEP

It would seem, however, that the conquistadors were incorrect in stating, as did Cieza de Leon, that the treasure of the Incas was hopelessly lost and that the descendants of the Incas "know not where to find it." Several legends, handed down over the centuries, appear to speak to a system of inherited guardianship, whereby a select few among the living descendants of the Incas are chosen to watch over the treasure, and to keep it from falling into profane hands.

Harold Wilkins, in his *Mysteries of Ancient South America*, reports that he was able to read one such story, recorded by Felipe de Pomares, of a young, Peruvian gentleman named Carlos Inca, a descendant of royal blood. Carlos, so the tale goes, was a resident of Cuzco, and married to a certain well-to-do woman from Spain, Dona Maria Esquivel. And although he was ambitious, he could never do enough to satiate his wife's appetite for the finer things. Continually hounded, day and night, by his wife, he finally resolved to share with her his well-guarded secret in the hopes that it might silence her complaints.

One night, while everyone else was asleep, he led her outside, blindfolded. He purposefully walked her in circles, in an effort to disorient her, and then guided her down a short stairway in or around the fortress of Sacsayhuaman. There he removed her blindfold, and she was utterly astounded by what she saw.

She found herself standing in a chamber of ancient stone, filled to the absolute brim with the lost golden treasure of the Incas. Precious artifacts, golden and silver ingots, and solid gold, life-size statues of ancient Inca rulers were ranged about the room, blinding her with the light reflected from her husband's torch. Only one item is said to have been missing: the Punchau, or golden disk of the sun.

Harold Wilkins, in relating this fascinating tradition, states his opinion that Carlos Inca was one of the guardians entrusted with the secret of the lost treasure, and from him the responsibility passed to a successor.[1]

A second story, and one possibly derived from the above, tells of a certain Peruvian Brigadier by the name of Mateo Garcia Pumakahua, who in 1814, in an effort to impress his superior officers, escorted them blindfolded for a great distance through a subterranean channel underneath modern Cuzco. Arriving at the treasure vault, Pumakahua removed the blindfolds, and his superiors stared in wonder at the riches that surrounded them. Incredibly ornate, life-size silver pumas encrusted with precious gems, and an enormous amount of gold and silver bricks covered the walls of the little room. It was additionally reported that directly above them, it was possible to hear the bells from the cathedral of Cuzco ringing out in the Plaza de Armas.

Of course, there is no way of substantiating either of the preceding stories, but luckily, stories are not all we have. As far back as the early 1600s, there exist records of intrepid explorers who successfully penetrated the tunnels, and bore witness to their marvelous contents.

In 1624, three men – Francisco Rueda, Juan Hinojosa and Antonio Orve – entered the fabled Chinkana at Sacsayhuaman in search of the lost treasure of the Incas. They tied one end of a very long rope to their waists, and the other they left in the care of numerous witnesses who recorded their descent. After several days, the rope went slack, and they were never heard from again.

In the 1700s, two students were said to have entered the Chinkana via Sacsayhuaman, in the presence of a large group of onlookers. After several days and no contact, most gave them up for dead. Until, ten days after they had entered the tunnels, there was heard a pounding beneath the floorboards of the church of Santo Domingo, which presently stands atop the ruins of the Coricancha. The congregation, which was attending mass at the time, was terrified that the pounding was coming from the devil himself, trying to break through the floor and into the church. The attending priest quieted the parishioners, and ordering the floorboards removed, was shocked to see one of the students emerge from the depths, emaciated and half-crazed. Clutched in his hand was a single ear of corn, made of solid gold.

As incredible as it sounds, there is some direct evidence to lend credibility to this anecdote. In 1994, a Spanish author and explorer named Javier Sierra was told by the Prior of Santo Domingo that the story was indeed true, and that the golden ear of corn had been seized by the church, melted down, and crafted into crowns intended to adorn the statues of the Virgin and Child, located within the church itself. As Sierra himself tells it:

Javier Sierra

*The church of Santo Domingo, built atop
the ruins of the Coricancha*

The priest met me in his study a little before daybreak on March 21, in order to resolve the mystery of the golden corn.

"I'm only going to tell this to you, I will let you take photographs and ask questions on one condition," he warned, "That you do not reveal what I'm about to tell you until I am no longer here."

I accepted. [The priest] then unwrapped a small bundle on the table of his study in which two elaborately encrusted gold crowns had been protected.

"The 'choclo' that you asked about was melted down shortly after the death of the student and my predecessors used the gold we obtained to make these crowns for the Virgin and the Christ Child that we have in the church."

"And why are they not in the church with the images for which they were made?" I asked while I was admiring the gold wasted on them.

"They have been hidden a long time so as not to arouse the ambitions of treasure hunters."[2]

The priest also confirmed the stories of a tunnel that connected the Coricancha with the archaeological site of Sacsayhuaman, but went further, telling them "Your information is correct, but the tunnel in question extends much beyond Sacsayhuaman, since it ends in some place underneath Quito, in Ecuador."[3] We will return to this Prior, whose name was Benigno Gamarra, shortly.

A variation on the foregoing story, repeated by David Hatcher Childress in his *Lost Cities and Ancient Mysteries of South America*, tells much the same tale, but states that it was a lone treasure-hunter who descended into the tunnels, and that rather than emerging with one ear of golden corn, he emerged with two solid gold ingots.[4]

A third legend, which seems to combine elements of the previous two, is related by the early 20th century adventurer William Montgomery McGovern, in his *Jungle Paths and Inca Ruins*. He writes:

> Near [Sacsayhuaman] are several strange caverns reaching far into the earth. Here altars to the Gods of the Deep were carved out of the living rock, and the many bones scattered about tell of the sacrifices which were offered up here. The end of one of these caverns, Chincana, has never been found. It is supposed to communicate by a long under-ground passage with the Temple of the Sun in Cuzco. In this cavern is supposed, and with good reason, to be hidden a large part of the golden treasure of the Inca Emperors which was stored away lest it fall into the hands of the Spaniards. But the cavern is so huge, so complicated, and its passages are so manifold, that its secret has never been discovered.
>
> One man, indeed, is said to have found his way underground to the Sun Temple, and when he emerged, to have had two golden bars in his hand. But his mind had been affected by days of blind wandering in the subterranean caves, and he died almost immediately afterwards. Since that time, many have gone into the cavern, never to return again. Only a month or two before my arrival, the disappearance of three prominent people in this Inca cave caused the Prefect of the Province of Cuzco to wall in the mouth of the cavern, so that the secret and the treasure of the Incas seem likely to remain forever undiscovered.[5]

What McGovern reports regarding the closure of the tunnels by order of the Peruvian government is certainly true. The official version of the above story is documented in the *Seria Documental del Peru*. Here it was recorded that in 1923 a group of archaeologists and professional spelunkers working with the University of San Marcos in Lima, Peru, formed an expedition to explore the circuitous tunnels rumored to exist underneath Sacsayhuaman. The expedition was dubbed Team Espeologos. It was decided that half of the team members would remain above ground, in order to monitor the exploration's progress, and the other half, comprised mainly of the spelunkers, would descend into the cave system and proceed west, in the direction of the coast. After a few days, however, all contact between the two groups was lost.

It was only 12 days later that a single explorer emerged again at Sacsayhuaman, raving like a madman about interminable mazes of pitch black tunnels and booby-traps, the likes of which would give pause to any would-be adventurer. The man, in his panic-stricken state, was warned by his colleagues to keep quiet, lest he be pronounced clinically insane.

In 1927, four short years after the failed expedition and the same year that McGovern's book was published, the government of Cuzco ordered the entrance to the tunnels dynamited, and subsequently walled up, to prevent any other amateur explorers from losing their lives in the labyrinthine passageways.

But despite the best efforts of the Peruvian government, treasure hunters and aspiring adventurers have persisted in attempting to unravel the mystery of the subterranean tunnel system. In 1952, a joint French and American expedition of 12 explorers entered the caves via a small access tunnel they had discovered in the area of Sacsayhuaman. It was a full 15 days after they entered that French adventurer Phillipe Lamontierre emerged again from the same hole, suffering from malnourishment and exhibiting symptoms of the Bubonic plague, brought on by contact with cave bats. Lamontierre told witnesses that the rest of the team had perished in the dark depths of the underground shafts, with some falling into unfathomable abysses deep in the earth. As proof of his story, he carried with him a golden ear of corn, which was supposedly donated to the Archaeological Museum of Cuzco, although I can find no record of any such donation.

Yet another expedition was attempted in 1998, by Raul Rios Centeno, a member of the Peruvian consumer protection agency INDECOPI. After apparently bribing the guards around Sacsayhuaman with a generous sum, Centeno and his little team entered a small chamber which connected to the main branch of the tunnels via an entrance which they discovered within the archaeological site. They began to advance in the general direction of the main tunnel system, utilizing a RAD-2 X-Ray Filter to take X-ray and infrared images of the walls as they did so. Unfortunately for Centeno, the chamber quickly diminished in height to a mere 92 centimeters, preventing the team from continuing on to the central shaft, and forcing them to turn back. However, the X-ray images revealed something puzzling. According to post-expedition analysis, the walls of the connecting chamber did not reflect infrared rays, due to being coated with an unknown type of metal, comparable to lead. Could this be evidence of ancient high technology at work? Centeno's findings constitute a genuine mystery, and until the tunnel system is opened up to scientific evaluation, likely will remain so.

[1] Wilkins, Harold T. *Mysteries of Ancient South America*. Kempton, Ill:
Adventures Unlimited Press, 2005. Print. pp.163-164
[2] Sierra, Javier. "First Report: Inca Gold – In Search of the Ultimate Inca
Treasure." The Official Graham Hancock Website. 2001.
<http://www.grahamhancock.com/forum/SierraJ1-p4.php>
[3] Coppens, Philip. "The Gold of Gran Paititi." PhilipCoppens.com.
<http://www.philipcoppens.com/granpaititi.html>
[4] Childress, David H. *Lost Cities & Ancient Mysteries of South America*.
Stelle, Ill: Adventures Unlimited Press, 1986. Print. p.64
[5] McGovern, William M. *Jungle Paths and Inca Ruins*. New York & London:
Century Co, 1927. Print.

4

THE BOHIC-RUZ
EXPEDITION

This brings us to what is perhaps the most well-documented of all modern excavations of the tunnel system, that of Spanish archaeologist and explorer Anselm Pi Rambla.

His story begins back in 1982 when, on a visit to the ancient capital city of Cuzco, he and his traveling partner Francesc Serrat stopped in for a look at the Coricancha. They had heard tales of the tunnel system, and wanted to see for themselves if there was any truth to the rumors.

In the 1950s, following the destruction of the church of Santo Domingo by a violent earthquake, the church was rebuilt with wooden hatches in the floor, protecting Inca ruins beneath and allowing easy access for future archaeologists. Being an academic himself, Pi Rambla was able to convince the abbot of the monastery to allow him to descend into the crypts beneath the church via one of these floorboards, for research purposes.

After descending a short flight of stairs into one of the crypts, the abbot switched on a dusty light and removed a few loose stones to give Pi Rambla a glimpse of something he would never forget. Beyond the rubble, there stood an enormous tunnel, in megalithic style, running off into the darkness. Pi Rambla relates:

> Behind the wall our host showed us a great tunnel...The chamber must have been very wide and was pitch black. The abbot wouldn't let us go farther and made us leave.

The old Father gave no reason for not permitting Pi Rambla and his partner from entering the passageway. Perhaps he was fearful of being held responsible should the archaeologist, like so many explorers before him, go missing. Perhaps he thought better of exhibiting the tunnel to profane eyes. Or perhaps, as some have suggested, he was protecting a well-guarded Church secret from inquisitive outsiders. But then, why show the tunnel to them in the first place?

Whatever it was that stopped the priest, Pi Rambla became a man possessed. He resolved to not rest until he obtained permission to enter the crypt and begin the first scientific excavations of the long lost labyrinth of the Incas. It would be 18 years before his dream could be realized.

In 1999, Pi Rambla negotiated a deal with then-Prior Benigno Gamarra - the same priest who had told the fabulous story of the golden corn to Javier Sierra in 1994 - to explore the tunnel system running underneath the Coricancha, and for thousands of miles to every corner of the Inca Empire.

Father Gamarra, apparently sympathetic to adventurers, told Pi Rambla that the Church had long known of the tunnels, but had decided to keep them a secret, not only for fear of jeopardizing the existence of the monastery, but also in hopes that they might one day profit from discoveries made within the subterranean chambers.

Anselm Pi Rambla

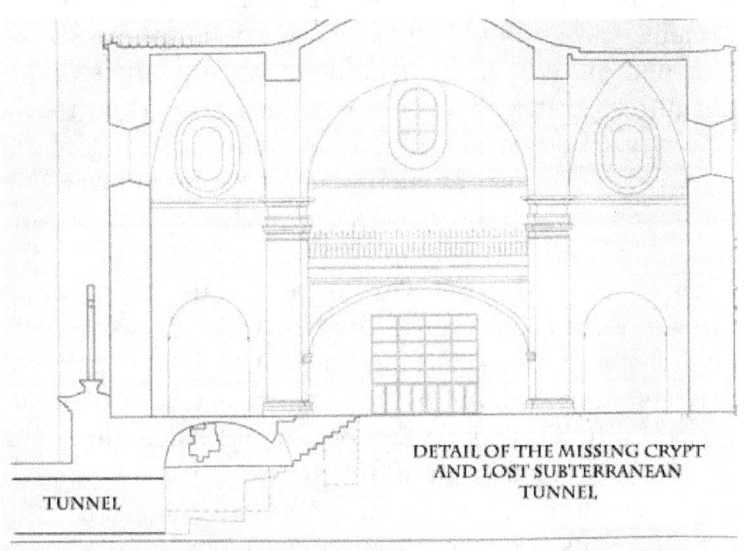

DETAIL OF THE MISSING CRYPT
AND LOST SUBTERRANEAN
TUNNEL

TUNNEL

Location of the mysterious tunnel,
according to Pi Rambla

Gamarra went on to tell Pi Rambla that in 1940, a Dominican brother had entered the chinkana beneath the church and traveled underground, in darkness, for a distance of roughly a mile before reaching a point directly underneath Sacsayhuaman. There he had discovered vast piles of gold, as well as statues of the ancient Incas, but had touched nothing, and had returned the way he came. Since that time, the story of the tunnel system had passed from Prior to Prior as a closely guarded secret. However, there exists a recently discovered document which would seem to indicate that the Priors knew of the tunnels for much longer than that.

In 2010, a parchment was uncovered in the Archivo Regional del Cuzco by Peruvian historian Ronald Valenzuela Camala that dates to the year 1642. The document details the particulars of a contract between the Prior of Santo Domingo and a Catholic treasure-hunter, seeking the lost gold of Atahuallpa. The contract stipulates that if the treasure hunter entered "the chinkana located within the Convent in order to search for its treasures," he would have to "pledge to donate to the convent half of all [he] might find." He was required to do this as an "offering" to the Church. And it was only under these conditions that the Prior would consent to admit the man to the tunnel system "by said chinkana."[1]

Gamarra next agreed to allow Pi Rambla access to the crypts, and permitted the explorer to use a crowbar to pry open one of the wooden hatches on February 14th, 1999, when the church was closed to the public. The original hatch that Pi Rambla had entered in 1982 was no longer visible, and seemed to have been covered over with tiling in the interval. Pi Rambla also found that the crypt into which he'd originally descended had mysteriously disappeared, which further aroused his suspicions that the Dominicans were purposefully hiding something of great historical import for the human race.

Father Gamarra, however, seemed the one priest concerned with the truth of the tunnel system. He informally agreed to allow Pi Rambla to officially excavate in search of the subterranean passageways, as long as the Peruvian government provided assurances that if anything of value were to be found, nothing would be immediately seized, and that the church of Santo Domingo would continue to exist.

In July of 2000, an official contract was drawn up between Anselm Pi Rambla, Father Benigno Gamarra as an official representative of the monastery, and the Peruvian government, outlining all of the conditions that Gamarra had insisted upon. Dubbed the Bohic-Ruz excavation, the project was to be funded by Texas financier Michael Galvis with an initial advance of $760,000, just to get things going. Honest, scientific exploration of the legendary tunnel system could finally begin in earnest.

But then something odd happened. One month after finalizing the agreement with Pi Rambla, Father Gamarra was unexpectedly replaced as Prior and sequestered in a convent in Arequipa, a Peruvian city roughly 14 hours south of Cuzco. The man who replaced him, a Father Hector Herrera, was far less sympathetic to the goals of the dig. In fact, Herrera seemed to be purposely delaying the excavation's progress, restricting access and refusing to allow the archaeologists to work on more than one section of the church at a time.

On August 19th of 2003, Herrera issued a memorandum effectively nullifying the contract previously signed by Father Gamarra. He additionally leaked a story to the Peruvian newspaper, El Comercio, accusing Pi Rambla and his team members of undermining the structural foundations of the church of Santo Domingo. Pi Rambla was forced to pack up shop and leave, without exploring the enigmatic tunnels.

However, prior to his departure, Pi Rambla was able to commission scans of the church's foundations using Ground Penetrating Radar (GPR). The images resulted in several interesting discoveries. The team determined that the crypt which Pi Rambla had originally entered in 1982 did, in fact, exist, and had simply been deliberately walled up and disguised at some point in the 18 years that had elapsed since then. But, more importantly than that, they were able to finally substantiate the legends surrounding the existence of the tunnel system.

The team was overwhelmed to discover a large subterranean passageway, detected beneath the altar of Santa Rosa de Lima, that continued in an undeviating straight line in the direction of the main Plaza of Cuzco and Sacsayhuaman beyond. According to Jordi Valeriano, a physicist working with the excavation team:

> Beneath the altar of Santa Rosa, about four or five meters down, we located a cavity two meters wide that we believe can be the entrance to a great tunnel.

Could it be that the mysterious tunnel system not only connected Sacsayhuaman to the Coricancha, but also featured access points along the route, perhaps at the Convent of Santa Catalina and the Cathedral of Cuzco in the main square, as well as at the church of San Cristobal built just below Sacsayhuaman itself? Pi Rambla

The altar of Santa Rosa de Lima

certainly believes so, as he indicated in an interview with EFE News:

> All of these buildings are in perfect astronomical alignment, which confirms that ancient Peruvians also guided their constructions by the location of the Sun, the Moon and the constellations…[Pi Rambla] explained that this [tunnel system] would involve a "Pre-Inca Citadel" belonging to a culture that has yet to be considered.[2]

The archaeologist went on to state that if such a citadel does indeed exist, he believes that it could be located at a depth of more than 300 feet below the surface of the earth!

That there might exist entrances to the tunnels at the various churches and cathedrals located between the Coricancha and Sacsayhuaman is not so far-fetched. After all, it is a well-established fact that the Spanish erected their Christian edifices on top of the ruins of Inca palaces, which in turn may have commemorated even older structures.

The GPR had additionally revealed numerous other cavities underneath the church of Santo Domingo and the surrounding area. Beneath the portion of the Coricancha referred to as the "Temple of the Stars", at the same depth as the tunnel, the GPR detected what appeared to be ruins of an ancient temple that may well predate the Incas, and be linked in some way to the subterranean passageways.

Furthermore, the GPR detected a number of arched doorways and structures buried underground toward the side of the church, which may or may not be associated with the tunnel system. Unfortunately, Father

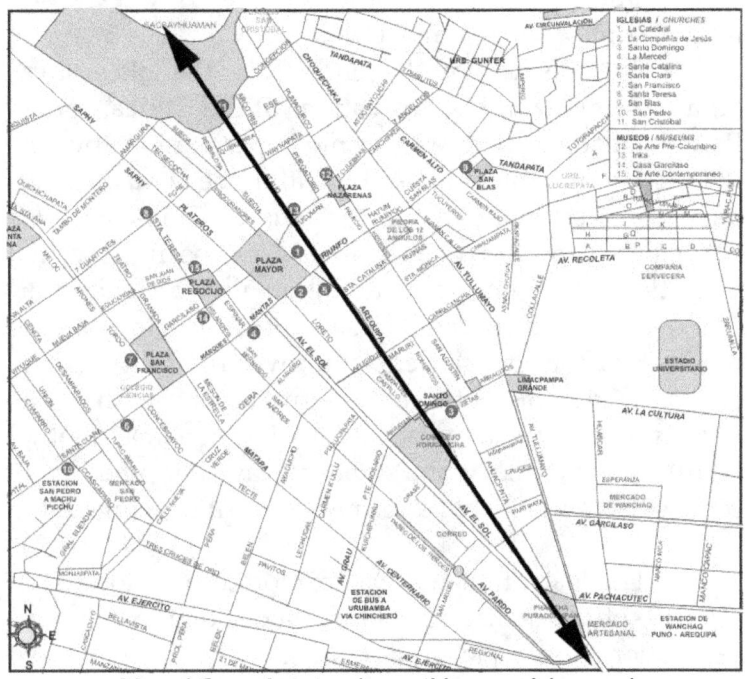

Map of Cuzco depicting the possible route of the tunnel

Herrera moved to expel the team from the premises before they were able to carry out any further investigations, with the result that the GPR scans still remain somewhat of a mystery.

But this is not the end of Pi Rambla's story. Simultaneous with his excavations at the Coricancha, Pi Rambla had also been granted permission by the Peruvian government to search within the archaeological park of Sacsayhuaman for the elusive Chinkana. One particular feature of the park had long been associated with the fabled entrance, and that was an enormous boulder nicknamed the "Tired Stone," located toward the back of the site, carved with mysterious shapes and staircases, reminiscent of a modern Escher painting. The rock is still held to be sacred to Pachamama (mother earth) by the locals, who regularly leave her offerings of coca leaves and chicha (a fermented corn beverage) atop it.

The lost Chinkana was rumored to be located at the base of the rock, and Pi Rambla decided to begin his excavation there. He and a team of 16 men worked tirelessly in removing 20 tons of sludge, debris and water, digging below the stone to a depth of 18 meters toward the center of the rock, until they could continue no further. Though in the course of the excavation they found several burial sites, the team determined that if the Chinkana was to be found in the area, it was not, as was widely believed, directly beneath the boulder itself.

Pi Rambla was unable to carry out any further excavations before operations were discontinued by order of the Peruvian government. The mystery of the Chinkana, and the labyrinthine tunnels said to wind throughout the limestone bedrock of modern Cuzco, persists.

[1] See a facsimile and translation of the document here:
http://www.koricancha.net/documentoinedito.html
[2] Whitehead, David. *CryptoQuest Field Guide to the Mysterious Tunnels and Caves of South America.* 2008. Print. p. 8

5
ZONA X

Just up the road from Sacsayhuaman, about 10 minutes by car, is another archaeological site of which most people have never heard. Located off the road and away from prying eyes, "Zona X," as it has been cryptically dubbed, represents a genuine mystery. Its original purpose is entirely unknown. Built in the same megalithic style as Sacsayhuaman, the little site boasts yet another marvel: tunnels. At least 30 tunnels, some running for several yards through the hillside before coming to an end, are known to exist next to these little-visited ruins. A number of them bear clear signs of being man-made, with niches or windows carved directly into the rock face of the tunnel walls.

Often, guides will regale the occasional visitors with stories of secret branches of the tunnels, mysterious disappearances and chambers full of gold. One such story is of a group of three boys who, hundreds of years in the past, managed to enter one of the tunnel branches. They wandered for days, two of them dying in the process, until just one boy emerged from an access point near the center of town, carrying the ubiquitous two golden ingots in his hands. These ingots, according to some, were then melted down and turned into the crowns which adorn the statues of the Virgin and Child in the church of Santo Domingo today. This is, of course, a variation on the story told to Javier Sierra by Father

Benigno Gamarra in 1994. Whether there is some truth to the legend, or if it simply derives from Gamarra's tale is open to speculation.

Another story, told by author Ricardo Gonzalez in his 2002 book *The Cosmic Legacy*, published and distributed exclusively in Peru, recalls the strange, sparking balls of light that he witnessed in the darkness of the tunnels of Zona X. As he tells it:

> I moved one meter, and suddenly I noticed some "sparks" coming out of everywhere. They were small, like the petals of a rose, and emitted a brilliant white light. I immediately felt a strong energy, and it seemed that the cave "disappeared." To make sure I was not imagining anything, I stepped back, and everything vanished as if by magic.[1]

Balls of white light are frequently associated with electromagnetic fluctuations, which in turn are known to be capable of inducing altered states of consciousness. Could it be that a feature of certain tunnels or areas at Zona X is increased electromagnetic activity? Shamanic practitioners still meet there to ingest hallucinogenic drugs and cross the threshold between this world and the next. Might Zona X be associated with an entrance to another world partly because of an unidentified electromagnetic anomaly?

Interestingly, the phenomenon of the white lights and their association with the subterranean tunnel system of the Andes is not confined solely to Zona X. It has been encountered at the ancient citadel of Tiwanaku in Bolivia, from which the Inca claimed to have originated, as well as at that most famous of all Peruvian sites, Machu Picchu.

The ruins of Zona X

One of the many tunnel entrances found in the area

[1] Gonzalez, Ricardo. "Un Ser de Luz en Cusco." <u>Rahma es Amar</u>. 2002. <http://www.rahmaesamar.com/portal/docman/ricardo-gonzalez-articulos/index.php>

6

AN UNBELIEVABLE DREAM

In 1911, a bookish, wiry little man in search of a lost Inca holdout made his way up the treacherous slopes of Machu Picchu Mountain, trailing behind an 11-year-old Quechua boy named Pablito Alvarez who acted as his guide.

Hiram Bingham was at that time a Yale lecturer on South American history, and he had traveled deep into the inhospitable, tropical wilderness of Peru looking for Vilcabamba, the last city of the Inca, from which they had made their final stand against the invading Spanish in 1572.

Cutting through the dense jungle that enveloped the mountain side, after hiking for two hours and ascending roughly 2000 feet, Bingham was shocked to be met by two indigenous farmers carrying gourds of cool water. They gave him the refreshments and were happy to show him their plots of land, which consisted of several ancient terraces that they had cleared and replanted. They informed Bingham that they had been living there for a full four years, undisturbed by nosy outsiders and the Peruvian government. Says Bingham:

> It seems that two Indian farmers, Richarte and Alvarez, had recently chosen this eagles' nest for their home…Here the Indians had finally cleared off and burned over a few terraces and planted crops of maize, sweet and white potatoes, sugar cane, beans,

peppers, tree tomatoes and gooseberries.[1]

Bingham and his guide continued up the mountain, seeing nothing more than remains of terraces for quite some time. Suddenly, and without warning, he found himself standing in the midst of the ruins, surrounded on all sides by some of the finest masonry and the most breathtaking scenery that he had ever witnessed. As Bingham tells it:

> It seemed like an unbelievable dream...It fairly took my breath away. What could this place be? Why had no one given us any idea of it? Even [my guide] was only moderately interested and had no appreciation of the importance of the ruins which Richarte and Alvarez had adopted for their little farm...Made of beautiful white granite, the walls contained blocks of Cyclopean size, higher than a man. The sight held me spellbound.[2]

He continues:

> Would anyone believe what I had found? Fortunately, in this land where accuracy in reporting what one has seen is not a prevailing characteristic of travelers, I had a good camera and the sun was shining.[3]

The site, entirely covered in thick vegetation, had to be cleared before serious excavation could be undertaken. And an elaborate series of perilously steep switchbacks were built into the sides of the mountain to allow for vehicular access. Hotels were built by the dozen in the nearby town of Aguas Calientes (or Machu Picchu Pueblo). Restaurants sprang up, tour packages were assembled, and that is how, in just over 100 years,

Machu Picchu has become one of the most visited sites of the ancient world. Tourists from all over the world stream in mad dashes to the forgotten ruins every day, in numbers totaling upwards of 1,000,000 per year.

But despite the site's popularity, the true purpose of the mountain-top citadel remains unclear. There are numerous competing theories, but the one most widely accepted is that Machu Picchu was built sometime around 1450 as a royal estate for the Inca Pachacuti. However, upon close examination, the evidence on which this theory rests is surprisingly flimsy.

The two documents that scholars have relied on to prove the "royal estate" hypothesis date to the 16th century, and make no explicit mention of any location named Machu Picchu. In fact, the mountain today known as Machu Picchu (meaning "old peak"), along with its neighbor Huayna Picchu ("young peak"), is never mentioned by any of the Spanish chroniclers. What the texts do record is that there existed a site known as "Picho," which scholars have theorized was an abbreviated version of the full name of Hiram Bingham's famous, lost city. This "Picho" was said to be located between Condormarca and Tambo, which would put it within the general area (200 miles) of Machu Picchu.

However, as has been pointed out by a number of critics, the name "Picho," which means simply "peak," is used throughout the conquest-era documents in reference to innumerable places. One such "Picho" was mentioned as the name of one of the sacred hilltops just north of Cuzco. There can be absolutely no way of knowing whether or not any of the numerous locations referred to as "Picho" by the Spanish correspond to the ruins we know today as Machu Picchu.

Additionally, if are to assume that Picho is

An example of the contrasting architectural styles found at Machu Picchu

identical with Machu Picchu, then we must also assume that the Spanish knew of the site. Why, then, is there absolutely no evidence of a Spanish presence on the mountain in the archaeological record? There exists no indication of intentional destruction of any part of the ruinous citadel, which was practically the Spanish calling card, to which anyone who has visited Cuzco can attest. And certainly, given the guerrilla war which the Incas were waging against them until the end of the 16th century, if the Spanish had known of a mountain-top fortress, would they not have been eager to clear it of its inhabitants and pull it down brick by brick, to ensure that the rebellious Incas could not use it to their advantage?

But accepting for the moment that the Picho of the Spaniards is, in fact, our Machu Picchu, scholars point to a 16th century record of agricultural terrains that identifies the farm lands of the Urubamba valley (between Ollantaytambo and Chaullay) as belonging to Pachacuti and his descendants. Defenders of the "royal estate" hypothesis readily admit that "Picho" is not specifically mentioned in this record of agricultural terrains, but infer that

> ...since the terrains of the valley bottom belonged to Pachacuti, it is quite probable that the places at higher [altitudes] in the same zone were part of the royal estate of the king as well.

The above quote is taken from J. Rowe's *Machu Picchu a la luz de documentos de siglo XVI*, published in 1990. Despite the fact that Rowe makes it clear that he is making an assumption regarding the provenance of Picho, the paper is generally referred to as conclusive proof of the "royal estate" hypothesis.

Rowe, content with his inferences thus far, further conjectures that because the site may have belonged to Pachacuti, it was most probably constructed by him, stating:

> ...we can suppose that the Inca ruler choose Machu Picchu as a personal estate and as a memorial of war campaigns in the zone of Vitcos.

To be clear, the "royal estate" hypothesis rests upon three integral assumptions, none of which are in any way definitively proven or directly supported by archaeological evidence:

1) "Picho" is used in the Spanish records in reference to Machu Picchu
2) Picho belonged to the Inca Pachacuti, despite not being mentioned by name in the records
3) Pachacuti built Picho as his personal estate

It's plain that the "evidence" to which scholars point as incontrovertible proof that Pachacuti constructed Machu Picchu as a royal vacation home is, in fact, a house of cards built upon supposition and presumption.

And there are other problems. On the site of Machu Picchu, at least three architectural styles are clearly visible. The first and oldest consists of heavily weathered, sculpted bedrock. The so-called Funerary Stone located on the upper levels of Machu Picchu represents an excellent example of this building method. This architectural style is by far the most impressive, in part because whoever accomplished it made it look so easy. Numerous travelers have commented that the mammoth outcroppings of bedrock look as though they were simply molded out of clay by some master craftsman in the distant past.

The second style consists of megalithic blocks of stone, finely cut and hewn, and built atop one another like multi-ton puzzle pieces. These are reminiscent of the famous walls of Cuzco, fitted together so tightly that tourists cannot slip even a razor blade between them.

The third style, and clearly the most recent, is made up of smaller, roughly hewn bricks held together mostly by a clay compound similar to mortar. Often times, the buildings constructed in this fashion seem to have been built to mimic the basic design and appearance of megalithic edifices immediately next to them, as though the architects were trying to reproduce something that they no longer understood.[4]

Historians would have us believe that all three of the above styles were produced less than one hundred years before the conquest by one man, the Inca Pachacuti. But this assertion absolutely defies logic. These architectural styles are so undeniably different from one another, and so clearly distinct, that they're readily apparent to most people who visit the site with an attentive eye.

Could Machu Picchu have been inhabited by at least three separate cultures over the centuries of its existence? And could it, in fact, predate the Incas by an untold number of years?

[1] Bingham, Hiram. *Lost City of the Incas: The Story of Machu Picchu and Its Builders*. New York: Atheneum, 1948. Print. p.150

[2] *Ibid*. p.153

[3] *Ibid*. p.154

[4] Alfredo Gamarra was the first to call attention to these dramatically different architectural styles in the first half of the 20th century. Jan Peter de Jong, a researcher from the Netherlands who worked with Alfredo's son Jesus in Cuzco for 13 years, currently maintains a website dedicated to advancing Gamarra's theories. For more information, see http://www.ancient-mysteries-explained.com.

7
THE DWELLING PLACE OF THE GODS

The oral history of Machu Picchu, as told by the natives of Peru, is very different from the stories recorded in textbooks. Hiram Bingham, after discovering the site in 1911, chose not to consult with the locals about its purpose or layout, but instead bestowed various names on different areas of the site according to his own theories and assumptions. Names like "Temple of the High Priest," "The Caretaker's House," and "Temple of the Sun" almost certainly have no relation to the original purpose of the citadel. They were culled directly from Bingham's imagination, though modern guides often neglect to mention that to their tour groups.

Even the name "Machu Picchu" properly belonged only to the mountain itself, and not the ruins atop it. The original name for the city, according to local tradition, was Yllampu, a Quechua word which means "the dwelling place of the gods."[1]

So if Machu Picchu wasn't built by Pachacuti as a royal estate, and the names that Bingham proposed have no relevance, what was the site's true purpose?

According to oral tradition, Machu Picchu was a medical experimentation center. As incredible as it sounds, the locals insist that in the past, members of the Inca royal family as well as various nobility would come to Machu Picchu for extended periods of time, where they would be treated with a mixture of coca leaves and poisonous snake venom, and that this serum would enable them to live unnaturally long lives, up to hundreds of years in length![2]

Interestingly, a derivative form of this serum seems to still be in use by natives of the Amazon jungle region. Professor Oscar Medina, a resident of Cuzco, recalls the following story:

> I know a 72-year-old man in the jungle, who is a tractor mechanic and travels great distances to earn his living. He is called every time forest tractors stall or have an accident, and they often do after several days' trip in a sparsely populated area. At his age, most people are retired, at rest, and telling stories to their grandchildren. But no, Victor Murayari, with all his vigor and youth, is an active model for all young people. In the crude oil extraction camps, he always participates in strength competitions, plays football, and swims in the river with the young ones...And do you know what he answered when I asked him about the origin of his incredible vigor? He said: "I owe it all to my viper juice."

According to Medina, this rural energy drink is supposed to made in a large jar, full of extremely potent cane liquor and six live vipers that are missing their rattles. The essence of the vipers is said to be slowly extracted by the alcohol over a period of 90 days, at which time the brew is considered ready for human consumption. Could this be a diluted remnant of an ancient medicinal practice, first perfected on the rugged slopes of Machu Picchu?

It was to Machu Picchu then, that the upper echelon of Inca society went to be rejuvenated in their old age. When the Spanish arrived on the continent, however, things changed.

The damage which the Spaniards inflicted by the sword pales in comparison to that wrought by the foreign diseases that they imported when they first stepped foot on South American soil. A study published in 1981 estimated that the indigenous population of the Inca Empire was reduced by a full 93%, due to the introduction of European pestilences like smallpox and measles. Huayna Capac (Atahuallpa's father), the high Inca himself, is generally thought to have succumbed to smallpox in 1528, just prior to the conquest.

When word of Huayna Capac's death reached the scientists working in Machu Picchu, they quickly realized the potential threat to Inca society that the new diseases posed. Their solution, according to local tradition, was to refocus their efforts on finding a cure to the foreign illnesses. But to do this, they needed to quarantine themselves somewhere that would be safe from infection. They chose the underground tunnels and temple complex said to exist below the ruins of Machu Picchu. After transferring the bulk of their supplies to the passageways running beneath the earth, they sealed themselves in, permitting only selected messengers to enter and exit the facilities, in order to stay informed of the events transpiring in the outside world.

The catacombs in which they concealed themselves are thought to run for untold distances throughout the tropical mountains of the surrounding environs, and to connect with the rest of the tunnels said to crisscross the entire Inca Empire. David Hatcher Childress, in his *Lost Cities and Ancient Mysteries of South America*, writes that on one visit to the little town of Sao Thome das Letras in the Brazilian state of Minas Gerais, he was told of a large entrance to a tunnel system north of town, which was said to extend for thousands of miles, all the way to Machu Picchu itself!

That there exist underground rooms and passageways at Machu Picchu, the purpose of which is unknown, is indisputably true. I myself have seen and photographed the blocked up tunnels on numerous visits to the site. One entrance to the subterranean passages is said to be located on the region's central mountain, called Putucusi. From this secret entrance, the cavernous tunnels are supposed to lead underneath the Urubamba river and empty into a vast temple complex located directly beneath the ruins of Machu Picchu. The temple, according to some, is still visited by the initiated even today, who there conduct rituals and ceremonies dating back to the Inca Empire, keeping the traditions of their ancestors alive.

Should you be lucky enough to find the right guide, you may have the privilege of hearing local legends of the tunnel system from the natives themselves.

L. Taylor Hansen, in her book *The Ancient Atlantic*, tells the story of a Sioux Indian chief named Shooting Star, and his visit to the fabled lost city. A guide told Shooting Star of ancient myths which speak of a mysterious giant race that assembled Machu Picchu in the far distant past. The Sioux chief took the guide aside, and privately asked him if Machu Picchu was the city of the thunderbirds. The guide responded: "It is the city of the bird of lightnings. Every street is a feather, but one does not see that is so unless from an airplane." Hansen recounts the rest of the conversation, quoting Shooting Star:

One of many descending staircases at Machu Picchu, all of which lead to rooms that have been blocked up or filled in

Putucusi

"Where are the caves where people lose themselves?"

"They are under the city. Some of the entrances are secret. Others are closed."

"Have you ever been down in them?" I asked.

He shook his head. "It is forbidden." That answer I expected, and he knew that I did. We smiled our recognition.

"Where is your tribe?" he asked.

"Thousands of miles to the north, through the United States and almost to Canada."

"It is well," he said, and we clasped arms in the ancient manner (grasping forearms above the wrists).

A few days later, after the ceremonial length of time, he brought an old man. I had expected him. Altogether there were eight of us. We spoke of legends and words. "I tell you, my friends, this is the land of our beginning, where we went from the old red land even before it sank, because this land is as old as the dragon land of the fire god."

The red land, according to Hansen and numerous mythologies worldwide, was the original homeland of all peoples that was destroyed or sank into the sea, much as Atlantis.

The tunnels at Machu Picchu, like those at Zona X, also seem to be home to interesting electromagnetic and/or paranormal phenomena. Andrea Mikana-Pinkham, tour director at Sacred Sites Journeys, recounted an eerie tale of one man's experience inside the legendary tunnels. According to Mikana-Pinkham, a guide on an early trip she took to Machu Picchu told her that he had penetrated the tunnels via one of the secret entrances located on site, along with several archaeologists. The members of the group had roped themselves together, so as not to get hopelessly lost in the labyrinthine passageways. Minkana-Pinkham's guide brought up the rear. They hadn't proceeded very far, when the guide looked to his left at one of the adjoining tunnels and saw, in the darkness, an enormous ball of orange, glowing light. He was tempted to break away from the group and investigate, but he was unsure of himself, and feared the possible consequences. The tunnel entrance has since been closed, and her guide has been unable to return.[3] Just as at Zona X, are these unexplained glowing orbs a product of strange, electromagnetic anomalies deep beneath the earth? Or could it be something much more otherworldly? We'll return to this subject in a later chapter.

According to the oral tradition, after sealing themselves in the caves, the scientists of Machu Picchu set about finding a cure for the imported diseases. They had only worked for a short period of time, however, when word reached them of Atahuallpa's capture at the hands of the Spanish, and his subsequent execution. They recognized this as the end of their Empire, and decided to abandon Machu Picchu. They destroyed what they couldn't take with them, and their last act before leaving was to release the hundreds of venomous serpents from which they had concocted their miraculous serum. The medical staff retreated into the jungle, perhaps to join the survivors of the conquest in the legendary city of Paititi, the Inca citadel of gold. Is it a coincidence that, as is recorded above, natives of the jungle today make use of fermented vipers as a kind of primitive energy drink?

Interestingly, Hiram Bingham records that on the way to Machu Picchu Mountain, he was told that the place was infested with deadly snakes:

On the road we passed a snake which had only just been killed. [My guide] said the region was the favorite haunt of "vipers." We later learned the lance-headed or yellow viper, commonly known as the fer-de-lance, a very venomous serpent, capable of making considerable springs when in pursuit of its prey, is common hereabouts.[4]

Interestingly, the fer-de-lance serpent caused numerous problems during Bingham's excavation of Machu Picchu, sometimes taking the lives of the laborers who were working to clear the site.[5] Could this be why, despite knowing of the site, few locals dared to set foot in the ruins? Might the mountain-top citadel have gradually come to be perceived as taboo due to the presence of the poisonous vipers?

The oral tradition, though admittedly unverifiable, is most interesting, as it narrates a vision of the past markedly different from that which we are taught in school.

1 Foerster, Brien. "A Tale Of Two Lost Cities: Machu Picchu and Choquequirao." The Official Graham Hancock Website. 2011.
<http://www.grahamhancock.com/forum/FoersterB7.php?p=2>

2 For general substantiation, see: Foerster, Brien. *Inca Footprints: Complete Guide To Cusco And The Sacred Valley Of Peru*. Lima: Peru. 2011. Kindle file. p. 160; for futher information, see: Medina, Oscar. *The Enigma of Machu Picchu*. Peru: Milenium Editores. 1998.

3 Personal correspondence

4 Bingham, *Lost City of the Incas*, p. 149

5 Foerster, "A Tale of Two Lost Cities,"
<http://www.grahamhancock.com/forum/FoersterB7.php>

8
THE BUILDERS

So, if the tunnels exist, then who built them? Neither the Spanish chroniclers nor modern historians have been able to agree on who should be credited with the construction of the fabled labyrinths. As we've seen, some of the chroniclers were inclined to attribute the subterranean chambers in which the last of the Incas are said to have deposited their precious hoard to various Inca rulers.

Father Martin de Morua, in his 1616 *Historia general del Piru,* wrote that the Inca Tupac Yupanqui (grandfather of Atahuallpa) was responsible for the construction of the tunnels. Whereas, the Jesuit chronicler Father Agnelio Oliva, writing some 50 years earlier, asserts that Huayna Capac, the father of Atahuallpa, was the builder of this vast maze of subterranean roads that spanned the empire.

As some modern authors have mentioned, however, the relatively rudimentary tools available to the Incas would not have been sufficient to complete so grand a project, particularly if the rumors of the size of the tunnel network are to be believed. Not to mention the fact that Tupac Yupanqui only began his reign in 1471, a mere 60 years prior to the arrival of the Spanish. Even if we were to assume that he had embarked upon the mammoth undertaking in his first year, to dig, cut, hew, and clear the stone and earth required to complete a tunnel system upwards of 3000 miles in length (conservatively) in a 60-year period would have required mobilizing, coordinating and sustaining a workforce the size of which would have been historically unprecedented, and there exists simply no evidence of such a mobilization.

There have been numerous suggestions made by modern alternative historians as to who (or what) was responsible for the construction of the tunnel system. Proponents of the ancient alien theory, like Eric von Daniken in his *Gold of the Gods*, predictably attribute the tunnels to an alien race that colonized our planet long ago. Of course, like most of the theories von Daniken presents in his books, there's little direct evidence to support an extraterrestrial hypothesis, and the few anecdotes that he produces to lend weight to his claims have been shown to be wholly or partially fabricated.

There is, however, the issue of the glowing balls, so often associated with the tunnels. Balls like the ones described by visitors to the subterranean chambers are associated today with phenomena that most believe have some kind of alien origin. Some even claim to be able to communicate with the balls, to speak with them, as though they're living beings with an agenda and a purpose. The balls appear by the thousands at crop circles, ancient megalithic stone constructions, and temples in Egypt, Mexico, North America and elsewhere. As ludicrous as it sounds, is it possible that the glowing orbs are actually an attempt by ancient, vanished races or even alien beings to contact us?

Other authors have theorized that perhaps an ancient Atlatean race built the tunnels, in an attempt to escape a global cataclysm of some kind. Worldwide

Thousands of orbs photographed at a crop circle in Teton, Ohio

Glowing orbs photographed in Edfu, Egypt

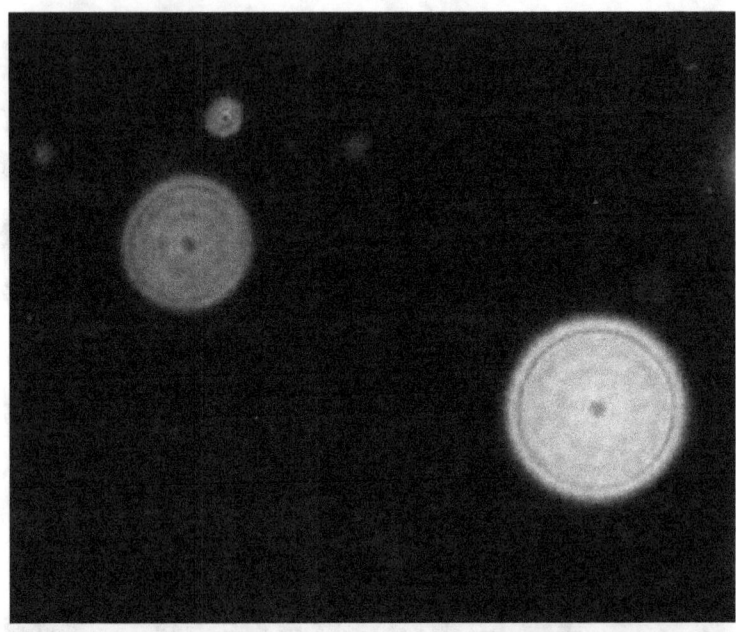

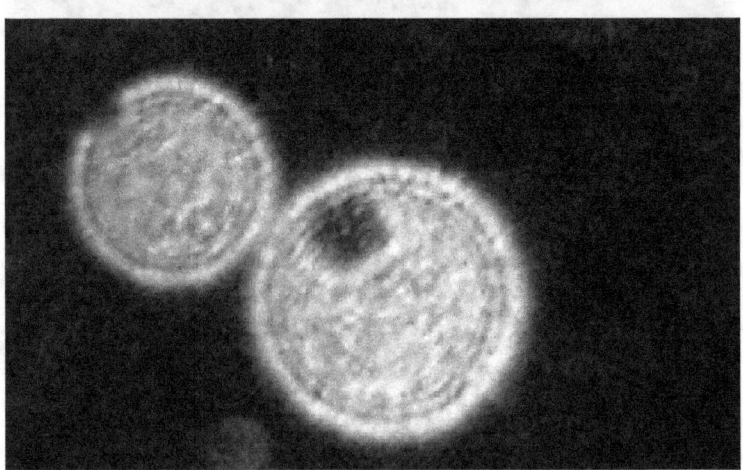

Two close ups of the enigmatic orbs

mythology certainly speaks to numerous cycles of destruction and creation, as well as lost lands and underground dwellings. Perhaps the races that constructed the tunnels still live beneath our feet, hidden from modern eyes.

Myths and local legends suggest that a race of giants was responsible for the construction of the tunnel systems, along with the rest of the megalithic monuments of Peru. Sarmiento de Gamboa, an early chronicler, was told by the residents of Cuzco that the world was originally inhabited by giants, who constructed cities, temples and citadels before being destroyed by Viracocha, the creator god:

> And when [Viracocha] created the world he formed a race of giants of disproportionate greatness painted and sculptured, to see whether it would be well to make real men of that size.

These giants lived in a world illuminated only by moonlight, until they rebelled against their creator and were destroyed in a calamitous flood which engulfed the whole world:

> ...[the giants] defied Viracocha, for which they were converted into stones and other things. The stone monuments at Tiahuanaco are a record of the memory of this event. Other giants were swallowed up by the earth and by the sea. Engulfing the land was a general flood called *unu pachacuti*, which means "water that overturns the land." It rained for sixty days and nights.[1]

Perhaps one tantalizing clue to the method of construction, if not to the builders themselves, is to be found in the records of Colonel Percy J. Fawcett, an adventurer and surveyor of the early 20th century, who disappeared in the jungles of Brazil while searching for a lost city that he identified only as "Z."

In his *Exploration Fawcett*, posthumously published, he writes of observing throughout Peru and Bolivia a certain variety of small bird, similar to a kingfisher, that makes its nest inside of small holes that dot mountainsides and cliff faces. One day, he remarked to a local that the birds were quite fortunate to find such perfectly suited nesting areas, "so neatly hollowed out – as though with a drill." The local, who had spent at least 25 years of his life in the jungle, was quick to respond:

> They make the holes themselves. I've seen how they do it, many a time. I've watched, I have, and seen the birds come to the cliff with leaves of some sort in their beaks, and cling to the rock like woodpeckers to a tree while they rubbed the leaves in a circular motion over the surface. Then they would fly off, and come back with more leaves, and carry on with the rubbing process. After three or four repetitions they dropped the leaves and started pecking at the place with their sharp beaks, and— here's the marvellous part— they would soon open out a round hole in the stone. Then off they'd go again, and go through the rubbing process with leaves several times before continuing to peck. It took several days, but finally they had opened out holes deep enough to contain their nests. I've climbed up and taken a look at them, and, believe me, a man couldn't drill a neater hole!

Noticing Fawcett's incredulity, the native went on to clarify:

Artist's rendering of a carving which appears atop the Gateway of the Sun in Tiwanaku. Many identify the individual depicted with Viracocha.

Colonel Percy Fawcett

No, I don't think the bird can get through solid rock. I believe, as everyone who has watched them believes, that those birds know of a leaf with juice that can soften up rock till it's like wet clay.[2]

A plant that can soften, even melt, stone? Fawcett, understandably, was ready to chalk up the story to the vivid imagination of the local population. But as his travels progressed, he continued to hear variations of the same story time and again. He was finally convinced of the truth of it when a fellow Englishman recited the following anecdote:

My nephew was down in the Chuncho country on the Pyrene River in Peru, and his horse going lame one day he left it at a neighbouring chacra, about five miles away from his own, and walked home. Next day he walked over to get his horse, and took a short cut through a strip of forest he had never before penetrated. He was wearing riding breeches, top boots, and big spurs— not the little English kind, but the great Mexican spurs four inches long, with rowels bigger than a half-crown piece— and these spurs were almost new. When he got to the chacra after a hot and difficult walk through thick bush he was amazed to find that his beautiful spurs were gone— eaten away somehow, till they were no more than black spikes projecting an eighth of an inch! He couldn't understand it, till the owner of the chacra asked him if by any chance he had walked through a certain plant about a foot high, with dark reddish leaves. My nephew at once remembered that he came through a wide area where the ground was thickly covered with such a plant. 'That's it!' said the chacarero. 'That's what's eaten your spurs away! That's the stuff the

Incas used for shaping stones. The juice will soften rock up till it's like paste. You must show me where you found the plants.' When they came to look for the place they couldn't find it. It's not easy to retrace your steps in jungle where no trails exist.[3]

And this is not all. Brian Fawcett, Percy's son, released an updated version of his father's book with yet another tale which seems to corroborate the oral tradition. Brian tells of a friend of his, who, along with several compatriots, had decided one Sunday to visit a few "Inca or Pre-Inca graves" to see if they could dig up anything valuable. After working throughout the day, however, all they'd managed to find was a small, clay jar that held about a quart of some strange liquid inside of it.

The men started drinking, and drinking predictably turned to roughhousing, and in the commotion somehow the jar was kicked over, and its contents emptied upon a large, flat-topped stone. No one minded, as they didn't expect to be able to sell it in the first place. But what happened next surprised everyone. As Brian's friend told it:

> About ten minutes later I bent over the rock and casually examined the pool of spilled liquid. It was no longer liquid; the whole patch where it had been, and the rock under it, were as soft as wet cement! It was as though the stone had melted, like wax under the influence of heat.[4]

Could the native accounts be true? Could there actually exist somewhere in the jungles of Peru and Bolivia a plant, the juices of which can turn stone to wax? As hard as it is to believe, it remains a living tradition among the native populations. Even Hiram Bingham recorded the tale in his Across South America:

> The modern Peruvians are very fond of speculating as to the method which the Incas employed to make their stones fit so perfectly. One of the favorite stories is that the Incas knew of a plant whose juices rendered the surface of a block so soft that the marvellous fitting was accomplished by rubbing the stones together for a few moments with this magical plant juice![5]

Are the above stories of giants and gods, lost civilizations and high technology simply colorful folk tales, or might they be diluted memories of real events that took place sometime in the distant past? Or perhaps the Spanish chroniclers were correct, and, defying all credulity, the Incas were actually able to carry out such a marvelous feat of engineering after all.

The reality is, authors and researchers can only play detective, utilizing the few clues left behind by the ancient cultures of the world to piece together the forgotten history of mankind. Until the subterranean chambers are penetrated by modern investigators and their contents exposed to the light of day, there's no way of knowing one way or another. The mystery remains.

---

[1] Steele, Paul R, and Catherine J. Allen. *Handbook of Inca Mythology*. Santa Barbara, Calif: ABC-CLIO, 2004. Print. p. 53

[2] Fawcett, Percy. *Exploration Fawcett: Journey to the Lost City of Z*. Penguin Group, 2010. Kindle Edition. pp. 106-107

[3] *Ibid*. p. 107

[4] *Ibid*. p. 425

[5] Bingham, Hiram. *Across South America*. New York: Houghton Mifflin, 1911. Print. p. 277